CHURCH PROOF

CHURCH PROOF

From Burned to Church Hurt Resistant

Yvette Currie, LMFT

Counseling San Diego Publishing

Published in San Diego, California by Counseling San Diego Publishing.

ISBN-13: 979-8988685500

Printed in the United States of America

For more information and to book this author visit www.counselingsandiego.org.

The contents of this book are for educational purposes. It is not therapy, nor is it meant to replace the advice you receive from your own treatment team.

This book is dedicated first to my parents, Paul Currie and Marie Currie. Without whom, I would literally not be here, but also! To whom I attribute so much effort to protecting and loving me. I've learned so much from you both. THANK YOU! And thank you, mom, for generously sharing your photos for use in this book.

Secondly, I attribute so many lessons learned from watching and knowing some giants in this world in a rich variety of backgrounds from the legal profession, to victim advocacy, to authors and speakers, pastors, and to those in psychology.

Often, you probably did not know I was watching. Thank you for your efforts to change our world and for adding to mine. Know that you are making impact, even when you aren't officially "trying."

"As for me, it matters very little how I might be evaluated by you or by any human authority."

1 CORINTHIANS 4:3

CONTENTS

INTRODUCTION

People don't enter through the church doors all fixed up. They come to church to get needs met and injuries mended. Pastor Nate Stewart of Greater Life Church San Diego frequently reminds congregants about the variety of attendees, from life long church members to those with a stamp on the back of their hands, from last night's club, smelling of last night's alcohol.

In addition, divorce, anxiety, and suicide occur among believers, regular church attenders, those in leadership, along with those attending irregularly.

While treatments for these concerns are proliferate, whether it's 12-step meetings or domestic violence shelters, an impediment to aiding those in church culture is the attitude that *it is not okay to admit* when these struggles are happening. Perhaps there's also the expectation of when one walks into church, the struggles will just go away.

Unaddressed wounds brought into the church will play out, in the church. The struggles will continue and may exacerbate, if they are not addressed and worked through, directly. Sometimes, these challenges will show up at the most unexpected moments, like an innocent church picnic.

The physical, spiritual, and psychological impacts of holding it all in are well documented. One of many, is an unnecessary taxing of the immune system. When the immune system is not functioning properly, this can lead to a host of issues, such as inflammation, infection, and diabetes. Addiction can be another outcome of suppression.

In a church panel I was invited onto, this year, multiple panel participants mentioned shame, as a barrier to divulging struggle. There are prohibitive and potentially paralyzing impacts of shame. Not only can the experience of shame be overwhelming, but the avoidance of it can become an entire lifestyle. Shame and vulnerability researcher, Brene Brown, goes into great depth on shame in her book *Daring Greatly: How the Courage to be Vulnerable Transforms the Way We Live, Love, Parent, and Lead* (2012).

Part of her discussion focuses on having the audacity to defy this shame; instead of hiding and shutting down, and avoiding this overwhelming feeling, getting back into "the arena." She describes the man in the arena as the one who's earned the credit, as he may stumble and get it wrong at times, but at least he is not sitting in the cheap seats, judging from the shadows, taking zero risk. Instead, he's out there trying, sweating and bloody and flawed and on occasion, getting it right.

We know those in a faith community have better resilience, from battling through loss, to depression, to isolation, than those without a community. We know prayer and worship provide not only spiritual benefits but physiological benefits, as well; for instance, singing together releases endorphins.

Experiencing church hurt, can, therefore, put us in what may seem like an impossible dilemma. Stay and continue to be injured or leave and miss out on vital community. It is not impossible. However, in order to continue and reap the benefits, it is going to be necessary to church proof your life and heart from church hurt.

Keep in mind, church hurt is omni directional. It can trickle from leadership to the church goer and from the church goer toward other church goers. Church goers may also internalize hurt or hurt church leaders. Families tend to get the brunt of all of it.

Fracturing off, alone, in silence, offended, resentful, and gossipy is a condensed formula for how to maintain church hurt.

Expect challenges to emerge within church, *because* it is church; a melting pot of harmed, healing, and hurting humans. In so expecting, you'll be more prepared to meet these challenges effectively.

Fortunately, it is possible to arrest the harms of life's storms, refuel, establish healthier patterns, and transform these struggles into something resilient. Entering in to this process, has got to be intentional action. It won't *just happen* by saying you desire it to be so.

This is a benefit of *open* strugglers gathering together. This allows normalcy around disclosing pain and the desire to heal. It can allow a realm of possibility to open up, for specific assistance and intervention. It can help destroy the shame, that tends to fester when we are nursing our injuries alone, in secret.

Credit: Marie Currie via MarieCurrie1@gmail.com

It can be quite refreshing to learn we are not alone, however, and to observe others getting to the other side of struggles, which may be quite similar to our own.

This process, I see, as the antidote to church hurt. It is believers gathering together, pulling together, supporting each other, addressing concerns with one another, and getting through to the other side, together.

* * *

PROLOGUE

The foundations for the suggestions within this book include: scripture, psychological research, case studies, therapeutic examples, interviews, anecdotes based on real people and composites, and church experience. In addition, resources included range from a concentration camp survivor to a Navy Seal to Yoda.

When synthesizing the data, provided throughout these pages, be certain to run it through your critically informed opinion. No other mind on earth is quite like yours.

It is my intent you'll emerge from this reading, with a wiser and more discerning perspective, on not just your church experience, but on all of your relationships. That you'll feel more equipped for whatever might be thrown your way. That it might help uncover some unspoken concerns and provide a path forward to addressing them, healing from them, and emerging stronger.

That you would not feel compelled to leave an otherwise helpful environment, believing self preservation to be your only option. Nor that you would remain and stay silent out of intimidation. My wish for you is if you choose to leave, you'll do so proactively and pivot at your discretion.

Ideally, you'll work the tools within these pages to advocate for the healthiest version of you *and* involve yourself within the healthiest fellowship, for you.

Credit: Marcio Antonucci via Pexels.com

CHAPTER 1: THE DISENCHANTING

"This is the only work God wants from you: Believe in the one he has sent." John 6:29

Jeremy was prepping for departure for Sunday morning service. He was tired and running behind schedule, after a late night up with a sick dog. He was slotted to be a greeter, that morning. Moving vigorously about the house, he struggled to locate a matching tie for his maroon shirt. Multi tasking, he spilled his coffee and experiencing frustration, raised his voice, intended for his wife and children to "get IN the car."

He was frazzled. He wondered why he was doing this, but dismissed the thought and ratcheted up his efforts just a notch higher. "Press" he told himself as he expelled a deep exhale.

On the way to church, he mashed the accelerator with aggression and weaved just a bit faster than the flow of other cars, in adjacent lanes. His wife, Jocelyn, looked over, furrowing her brow, gripping tighter to her door with one hand and looping her left hand behind her husbands seat back, she turned to observe her children in their belted harnesses behind them. Their (7) and (8) year old heads bobbing to and fro, with the swerves of the careening vehicle.

Jeremy turned the volume knob several clicks to the right, flooding the vehicle with Gospel music. *This* would help.

Jocelyn, annoyed with the unfolding events of the morning, edgily chirped, "Would you turn. the. music. downnnn?"

Jeremy simultaneously slammed on the brakes, as a car ahead abruptly stopped at an intrusive light. "Where did *that* come from?" He uttered. His patience was lost in the back somewhere, behind the bobbling heads of his children, as he loudly exclaimed "Can't you see, we are on our way to PRAISE THE LORD!"

* * *

God does not want worker bees buzzing around the hive with no thought or concern for their impact on others. When Oliver Wendell Holmes, Sr. stated "Some people are so heavenly minded, they are no earthly good," this may have been what he meant.

When pleas from family for attention and time are ignored and church tasks and attendance are prioritized, instead, or where promises are broken and forgotten, but instead kept strictly on Sunday mornings; it's time to reprioritize.

If you are a whirlwind of activity, especially when it comes to church involvement, but don't recognize yourself or why you are actually doing it, it may be time to slow down. It may be time to look at what's driving you and who conveyed to you, this is how it's done. This is how you do church.

Working to earn favor is a tendency that goes back to the Old Testament, wherein, rules and performance based outcomes dictated a favorable existence. We tend to be creatures of performance: for love, for grades, at work, and especially when it comes to religion. We tend to work harder and harder to "make" things happen, when in reality, we don't have the capacity to control outcomes. Fortunately, Jesus operates in grace and doesn't care for the performative.

When a person is depleted, there isn't a deep reserve to draw from, to extend generosity toward others. In Maslow's hierarchy of needs, basic self preservation takes precedence above all else: such as food, clothing, and shelter. In very simple terms, you can't give what you don't have. If your enthusiasm is zapped, remember, God is looking at the heart and the cheer in the giving. Otherwise, he doesn't want it.

Credit: Ric Rodrigues via Pexels.com

CHAPTER 2 : DISSONANCE

"Jesus answered them, 'Healthy people don't need a doctor - sick people do.'" Luke 5:31

The church is notorious for being a place where harm actually occurs, rather than the healing intended, as Jesus points out in the verse at the top of this chapter. In fact, it has become a place of gossip and judgment, and divisiveness, cliquishness, and exclusion; a place where some people actually feel very lonely. A common term for this is "church hurt."

Jesus set up a spiritual hospital on one end of the spectrum, as his intent for the church. The church as defined as an assembly of like minded individuals. However, it has, at times, traversed to the other end of the scale, becoming a place where actual abuse occurs. A radical departure from his original plan.

Recent reports cite people stopping church attendance, for a variety of reasons, including COVID. The impacts of COVID will be researched for years to come. One such impact is on community and connectedness. These are foundational to our thriving. People have become used to staying home. While people do continue to function, operating without a community, in today's culture of a 24/7 "news" cycle, isolating with toxic streaming data can be damaging.

We need each other for perspective, support, and hugs, among a plethora of other reasons. Feel good hormones, like oxytocin, are released into our systems during positive interactions. Oxytocin can contribute to mental health, such as lowering anxiety. Church can be a way to meet these needs. However, during negative interactions, stress hormones, like cortisol are released. Cortisol can adversely affect sleep and energy, among other areas.

The church needs to be a safe, sheltering, loving environment, in order to get those needs met. In the event that it is not, the hurt, as mentioned earlier, can be omni directional. We bring hurt inside the church community and we absorb and enact it between one another and we take it home to our families.

How are rumors and offenses handled within your church? Is the prayer chain a gossip mill? Remember in Matthew 18

> *"If another believer sins against you, go privately and point out the offense . . . if you are unsuccessful, take one or two . . . witnesses."*

This direct approach can be unbelievably scary for people.

However, the more able we are to note our blindspots and recognize our injuries, the more accurately and efficiently we can advocate and course correct. While we are all under construction, these skills can be developed.

Below are some observations where church related hurt has

crept in. It is not an exhaustive list, but it does examine some harms that differ from the culture at large. These are added layers of difficulty and complication that can be present among church goers.

Hurt From Within

In some cases, promoting the Good News is prioritized above all else, even over advocating for oneself to get healthy and healed, first. Additionally, exhaustion and resulting personal suffering are regularly revered in our churches.

All in the name of a God that never asked us to do so.

There also appears to be a disconnect between Biblical promises, such as living the abundant life, peace that passes all understanding, and the joy of the Lord.

In fact, some folks speak of just passing through this mortal coil of suffering here on earth, waiting until heaven to actually begin to live.

Despite Biblical promises to the contrary, these realities have taken root.

Some are fearful or hesitant to admit a disconnect between living day in and day out *demoralized* by trials and tribulations, rather than embodying the actual promises of God, as a *lifestyle*. As stated earlier, to discuss these areas openly can be quite scary. While we are often aware of the Bible verses addressing worry or joy, for instance, having a Bible verse quoted at us, in moments of distress, is not always helpful or desired. It can shut down the conversation.

Consider what you need most, in moments of uncertainty and pain. It may be an opportunity to ask for it, directly, with someone you truly trust. When people hesitate to share or ask for help, I've heard them describe fear of "being a burden." Later, when loved ones discover this hurt, they frequently wish they knew sooner;

they wanted to help. This is one way they show love and of this opportunity, they feel deprived.

On the flip side, remember this, when hearing another share their struggle and pain with you. Determine if that is the moment to dispense a Bible verse. When grieving, people often speak of platitudes thrown their way and that this feels unhelpful.

Sometimes, just sitting alongside, being present is all another person in suffering wants. There do not have to be perfect statements. The empathy and the company can go a long way.

When people open up to me in my office, the number one cited reason, is not because of my license or title, it's because they don't feel judged. This *we can all* practice.

Hurt From Religious Leaders

Another form of hurt, is people who came along, historically, and purported to have a special shortcut to God.

For example, enter an actual preacher I'll call "George." His teachings in the 1960s and 70s were strict and patriarchal and evangelical America appeared to devour his teachings like morsels of, frankly, Gospel. He *was* the Zeitgeist.

Verses mentioning "Spare the rod and spoil the child" along with the "Man is the head of the household" were selectively plucked from the pages of the Bible and placed as a central theme, as if ordered by God himself. These teachings were very convenient for the men in power, during those years.

And very inconvenient for the others.

Author Nancy Pearcey discusses in her book *The Toxic War on Masculinity: How Christianity Reconciles the Sexes* (2023) how some men took this concept to the extreme and layered over their destructive behavior with a "veneer" or title of "Christianity." She describes these as "nominal" or Christians in name only, using "headship" and "submission" as bludgeoning tools to get away with nefarious behaviors. These "nominal" types statistically have the highest rates of divorce and domestic violence.

The impacts of this one example, alone, are immeasurable, as there are reverberations in our culture, playing out decades later, in reality television.

These concepts taken to even farther extremes can be viewed in Alice Miller's *For Your Own Good* (1990). She describes discipline taken to the harshest end of the spectrum, as through that of authoritarianism. She posits, those Aryan youth who were disciplined so harshly "for their own good," were set in motion to become automatons as adults. Perhaps this was to avoid further punishment or they were operating in a trance, whatever the case, they were trained to submit to overbearing leadership, without question. They became controllable targets, willing to do anything for a cruel dictator, in Nazi Germany.

In *People of Lie* (Peck, 1983) M. Scott Peck details the most dangerous are the most well meaning, as the well meaning cannot be re routed, but will insist on moral high ground, exuding self righteous indignation no matter the cost to another human being. They may insist it is for your own good and they are good people. Even if the human standing in front of them, face to face, in abject suffering and pain, tears streaming down their face, is pleading for some compassion.

Credit: Philipp Deus via Pexels.com

While it would be easy to place blame on one person, to point fingers at cults and false teachers, it is important to note: well meaning swaths of people deviated together, taking another's word, about God's word, as God's word.

The red flags did not appear to be operational. If hurt is happening in Jesus' name. That is a red flag.

Hurt From Culture

A common struggle with *guilt* is another factor that regularly emerges amongst church goers. Believers have been promised, God tosses our sin as far as the east is from the west. He forgets and forgives our missteps, but we don't always seem to.

To be clear, we don't just pop out of the womb berating and judging ourselves harshly. We *learn* to do this.

The aforementioned theology stemming from 60 years ago, also directed it's focus toward the worthlessness of man, drawing from Bible verses about being as "filthy rags" and likened to "worms." If it is easier to embrace an identity of what is wrong with us and others, rather than to take a compliment, this is worth examining.

Self loathing can be likened to depression: which is unofficially defined as anger turned inward.

In American high school required reading, there are examples of religious extremism, such as *The Scarlet Letter* (Hawthorne, 1850), which describes Hester Prynne as judged by the town, visibly labeled, and identified as the worst of the worst. It also describes Arthur Dimmesdale as punishing himself with flagellation (whipping himself) alone in his closet, to atone for his wrong; their affair.

This book is but one example among countless others "educating" the culture about church goers. It was introduced reading into the American school system, shortly after it was published in 1850 and continues to this day. At very impressionable ages, we are taught a variety of extreme versions of what religion does to people; that it teaches us to hate ourselves and mercilessly judge others. Perhaps this perspective has seeped in to impact believers, as well.

Wise And Discerning

Jesus warns in Matthew 10:16

> *"Look, I am sending you out as sheep among wolves. So be as shrewd as snakes and harmless as doves."*

Applying this practically could look like taking the stance of an informed consumer. And in so doing, attending to where you've noted teaching or preaching or parenting or any leadership for that matter, that does not sit right with you.

The tiniest misguided direction of a plane flying even one degree off course, according to the aviation "1 in 60 rule" discusses the compounding effect into potentially catastrophic inaccuracy and mislocation. The culmination of the slightest aeronautical drift can translate into arriving in an entirely different country!

Practical application could be to attend to your church's mission statement, the fruit it's bearing, and whether intent matches the execution. Look for dissonance or congruence. Observe and notice whether your treatment matches with how your church and the Bible talk of treating people. If it's dissonant, is it safe to bring this observation up? To whom?

Think of this approach as taking the role of an advocate for yourself *and* still seeking God's wisdom. As Proverbs 4:21 states:

> *"Guard your heart above all else, for it determines the course of your life."*

Taking this missive to heart, could lead to questioning political leaders, Bible teachers, school teachers, and various authorities.

While the Bible instructs us to pray for those in authority, it does not instruct us to follow without question.

Uproot the narratives from time to time and assess the bulbs at the base or core premise.

Get curious.

Credit: Yvette Currie

In 1 John 4 we're told not to believe every spirit, but instead, to test the spirits.

In addition, sharpening those instincts could be assisted through the help of friends.

> *"As iron sharpens iron, so a friend sharpens a friend." Proverbs 27:17*

Zero Condemnation Status

If guilt is persistently beating you down, now is the time to take action and potentially learn new ways of handling old situations. Look at the facts surrounding your guilt, as a scientist collecting data, not as a judge. Challenge those feelings with facts and scripture. Uproot any false information you may be endlessly looping on. Catch it the moment you notice it and address it. Endless looping will not take you anywhere good.

Perhaps it's time to apologize. Perhaps, it's time to forgive yourself and to allow zero tolerance for self condemnation. Forgiveness impacts dopamine, cortisol, memory, heart conditions, depression, and anxiety. Perhaps this is why Jesus encouraged it.

Remember

> *"So now there is no condemnation for those who belong to Christ Jesus." Romans 8:1*

What is it going to take to get you to *zero-self-condemnation status?*

Assessment Tools

There's a series of questions called "The Work" put together by Byron Katie. It's based around (4) specific questions to disrupt the trance of automatic assumptions. My favorite concept she presents is essentially "do you know with 100% certainty that this is true?"

When you know what you are actually dealing with, then you can actually deal with the actual issue.

This could be strongly correlated with why Jesus said

> *"And you will know the truth and the truth will set you free." John 8:32*

Credit: Javon Swaby via Pexels.com

CHAPTER 3: OFF THE RAILS

We live in a fallen world. We've deviated far from the original plan; Adam and Eve in a garden of perfection, painless child birth, delicious fruit, and shamelessness.

Parent and guardian impacts have trickled down in a cumulative effect on to the next generation, and so on and so forth. In Exodus 34:7 it says

> *"...I lay the sins of the parents upon their children and grandchildren; the entire family is affected--even children in*

the third and fourth generations."

Perhaps they did not communicate productively through conflict, or drank to avoid uncomfortable feelings, or used violence to convey upset; because they never learned from their parents. Without learning the skills in childhood, nor deliberately seeking out alternative behaviors in adulthood, entire generations appear to be bereft of some core and basic skills.

Examples include conflict resolution skills, boundaries, and emotional regulation. And as established earlier, we bring ourselves, which includes our patterns, into the church.

Child Logic

We may be carrying around a set of unquestioned rules or assumptions in adulthood, based on norms established a very long time ago. However, core beliefs predicated on assumptions, that were formed in childhood, can be utterly false. Child rationale is quite different than adult logic. Part of the reason for this, is the child brain is not yet fully developed.

For instance, conflating the belief of if you were helpless back then, you are helpless now. This is false. A child has rudimentary tools to get through a difficulty. In childhood, we are all, essentially powerless. For instance, a child is small and typically unable to make impact in fighting back against adults. A child usually does not have a bank account and so cannot get an Uber to get respite from a threat.

Credit: CottonBro Studio via Pexels.com

A child hasn't developed complex emotional regulation, such as delayed gratification, or anger management. These instead, can, look like temper tantrums or sulking. This emotion fueled limbic system seems to run the show for awhile. Immediate gratification is so much more irresistable at this stage. The brain, particularly the prefrontal cortex, the executive (wise) functioning part of the brain, is not fully formed until 24 years old. This can also affect strategizing and problem solving in abstract ways.

In adulthood, situations may lead to *feeling* helpless, and be reminders of emotions during childhood. However, in stark contrast, the factors have completely changed. Some of the differences include: Access to support systems and allies, from attorneys, to therapists, to police officers, to support groups, to pastors, to friends.

Additionally, our bodies, bigger and stronger, can take us away from from threatening situations, or allow us to defend ourselves. Our fully developed brains have the capacity to choose from a wide variety of responses.

Frequently, in my role as a therapist, I will hear "Why didn't I just do something or say something. Instead, I just froze." In the animal kingdom, you'll find a variety of creatures that freeze, as if dead. They'll freeze and fall over, in an instinctual effort to save themselves and preserve their lives.

This is indeed another common reaction. Again, child tools are rudimentary, but also extraordinarily wise. Kids literally don't have much to work with. Whatever mechanisms your system implemented, you are here and you survived. Judging yourself for using particular tools and not others, will not serve you.

Critical Analysis

Examine assumptions based upon when you were younger, that may not be serving you, today, in adulthood. In childhood, we make agreements within ourselves and they aren't always stated aloud as mission statements. They can be like a personal pact or private contract. In one way or another, we decide and we stick to it.

We may leave it there, unquestioned for decades. These determinations can sound like, we will never let another person hurt us in the the same way, ever again. We will not be naive or will not cry. Or we decide to never trust a certain type of person, again. Without any nuance or adult brain analysis, these pacts can be rather limiting and rigid.

This may also lead to isolating, where if feels safer to just be alone. There are a lot of hurt and hurtful people out there. Wise protections are important.

However, avoidance, as a way of life, can put a severe halt on growth and chances for healing those long held injuries. Unchecked, these beliefs could calcify into concluding alone is your destiny or that people are just not safe. Locked inside a guarded tower, also means isolated alone in that protective tower.

Look at your life, now, and ask yourself if you have any long held agreements within yourself that may have saved you, when you were younger, at say, (5), and if they still make sense for you, now, at (35)?

Fight Flight Freeze Fawn

Fight or flight served us historically when we were physically threatened. For instance they'd strengthen and energize our predatory pursuit or survivalist retreat.

However, these levels of extremes to just get through one day to the next, when they are not actually needed, can set the body up for unnecessary chemical flooding (such as adrenaline or cortisol overload).

Think of extreme survival reactions as the body's fire alarms going off with enough intensity to respond to a fire or revving a powerful engine while simultaneously stepping on the brake. When there is no actual fire or life and death threat and these chemicals have nowhere to go, it taxes the body.

Credit: Rodolfo Clix via Pexels.com

Continue to confront your narrative with the truth and the facts. Attempt to assess with a neutral perspective, so you can logically examine, if the person at church triggering you, for example, is truly a physical threat. Assess if that person is actually able to threaten your survival needs, such as food, clothing, and shelter. Are all of your fire alarms and engines revving, at these levels, actually needed, in this instance?

When events occur, they are often neutral. We assign a narrative and a value, frequently of good or bad, from our individual perspective. That narrative is not always accurate.

The cognitive behavioral perspective suggests taking a look from alternative viewpoints and asking what might be motivating a certain person or event. It involves chiseling away at a presumptive narrative, through methods such as questioning whether another's behaviors are actually malevolent.

Write down (5) alternative explanations as to what *else* could be motivating the other person's behaviors or events. Notice if these different interpretations affect your mood.

Keep in mind that individuals are often focused on themselves and are reacting to events and people out of their own issues and uncertainties.

What if the other person is doing the best he can in that given moment, with the only tools he currently possesses? Might that change how defensive you get in response to that person? (Note, this is not a free pass for bad behavior. Dignity and respect are the baseline.)

And of course, if you'd like additional assistance, tap into a wise trusted person. This can give you fresh eyes on the subject.

* * *

CHAPTER 4: UNIQUE AND UNIFORMITY

"If the whole body were an eye, how would you hear? Or if your whole body were an ear, how would you smell anything?" 1Corinthians 12:17

Jeremy whirled into the church parking lot. He worked the family vehicle into a tight spot with a one handed whip turn. The steering wheel jolting and springing back in the opposite direction, spinning under and through his fingertips. The vehicle listed off to the side, momentarily straining the suspension, tipping a nod and winking to the adjacent vehicle on the left. At once, they unceremoniously reached their optimal destination, the closest parking spot to the front steps. *This* would save time.

The centrifugal force of the final arc left the two little ones mashed up against the side wall of the back set. Jocelyn looked back again to check on their whereabouts, capturing their stiffened postures, their child eye balls darting about. She also felt the pressure of a gravitational lurch off to the side, while noting the distinct dig of her seat belt into her shoulder and hip.

Before the bounce of the vehicle subsided, Jeremy had unclipped his seat restraint, swept up his Bible from Jocelyn's lap and thrown his door open. Two bounds from his (6) foot frame toward the front steps of the sanctuary, he was practically to the front door! He barked over his right shoulder "lock up would you? And hurry up, kids! We can't be late for church!"

His head swiveled to forward facing, just in time to prevent a body collision with Deacon Connor.

"Everything alright, brother Jeremy?"

Credit: Don Hainzl via Pexels.com

Jeremy stretched a smiled over his teeth and raised both eyebrows "Exhausted for Jesus. Praise the Lord from whom ALL blessings flow!"

* * *

Where did *this* personality come from?

If you find yourself habitually beaming on the outside, but crying on the inside, let this be the last day of anything performative for anyone, for any reason. This is easier said than done and there are steps to doing so. This is also not a suggestion to just *share it all* with everybody. This is a suggestion to find the real story within yourself and reveal it to at least one trusted human being.

There is a broad spectrum of reasons why people lock it down and show a curated version of themselves. People have also been known to go "grey rock" or intentionally hard to read, to protect themselves from certain personalities. Whether done intentionally or on autopilot, the results tend to be the same. This can be confusing for others and might result in keeping them at a distance.

The term "Christianese" and the concept of Christian peer pressure have a way of showing up, in churches, just as peer pressure shows up in the outside or secular world. Group norms tend to rub off on individuals, such as corporate speak or military speak. In some churches, there appears to be an "acceptable" way to express oneself. For some, this can seem insincere or fake.

As established earlier, people come in to church for a wide variety of reasons, from a wider variety of backgrounds. Trauma, culture, and upbringing, can all play a part in keeping what is happening inside a person very separate from what is shown on the outside. This shield or mask can be a very protective tool.

A long established set of family or cultural rules, may be contributing to various presentations. Keeping it in the family and not "sharing our business" is a powerful reason. Some children are forbidden to reveal family dynamics and norms and this can carry into adulthood.

Fear is also a powerful motivator. An example is fear of showing something "unacceptable" and getting judged or ostracized. Fear can slither in through all layers and facets of a church. Being in a position of leadership or of a certain age, may contribute to holding back. As once you reach a certain status, you are "not supposed to struggle with that!"

Keep in mind the concept of balance, middle ground, and nuance. If one end of the spectrum is total secrecy and the other end is "open kimono," neither extreme is healthy. Looking within and at how you choose to present require a curious, open-minded process, in order to actually make healthy changes.

At the same time, church culture is not corporate or military culture. Our personalities are designed distinct and unique, for a reason. The more unique the better. The more flare, the more of a display of the creativity of God.

> *"Don't copy the behavior and customs of this world, but let God transform you into a new person by changing the way you think...." Romans 12:2*

There will never be another you, nor has there ever been another you. No other human can occupy and accomplish precisely what you or I can. You are the only one, ever. So stop copying anybody else, in or outside the church. Neither on Instagram nor anywhere else.

If you are unsure of who is safe and trustworthy, listen to your internal alarm bells, and bounce your hesitation off of a counselor. Recall, in John 2, we're informed, Jesus didn't *just trust* people. And while being self protective can spare you some pain, remember, by essentially hiding out, others will be missing out on the blessing that is the actual you.

* * *

Critical Assessment

Take a moment to examine if you ever step into a different personality, when you step into church. Look at the impact this is having on you and the people around you. Challenge the fears, the scripts, the preconceived notions for stepping in to this persona.

If you've ever been tempted to streamline who you actually are into some uniformity of personhood, please look at this from a different perspective. This may be a briefly rewarding posture as it may provide more "holy" currency and, therefore, more acceptance, for awhile. While acceptance can be a powerful motivator, in the long run, the cost of your authenticity may breed exhaustion or resentment.

In addition, if your family has watched you transform from the at-home-persona into the church version of yourself, they may be wondering what alien took over your body. This could cost you trustworthy points, at home. When it comes to family and church, evaluate any underlying assumptions you may have, such as "my family will always be there. It's the church, I have to impress!"

Credit: Marie Currie via MarieCurrie1@gmail.com

CHAPTER 5: THE ACTUAL JESUS – UNAPOLOGETIC

> *"Then the disciples came to him and asked, 'Do you realize you offended the Pharisees by what you just said?' Jesus replied . . . 'so ignore them.'" Matthew 15:12&14*

Jesus is often portrayed as a wounded, meek, victim; whether through paintings or carvings or oft quoted Bible verses. However, the Jesus of the Bible was actually full of self possession, boundaries, power, and relentless loving, encouraging, and fighting for us.

> *"Who then will condemn us? No one - for Christ Jesus died for us, was raised to life for us, and he is sitting in the place of honor at Gods right hand, pleading for us." Romans 8:34*

He consistently focused on setting us all free.

> *"So if the Son sets you free, you are truly free." John 8:36*

Through his words, his role modeling, and his teachings, he provided for us the roadmap out of captivity.

In Hebrews 2:15:

> *"Only in this way could he have set free all who have lived their lives as slaves to the fear of dying."*

He also encouraged us to cultivate it and share it. Part of the reason why he may have focused so much on our freedom, is the fact that freedom is our abundant birthright. In other words, Jesus is *all in* for us and wants us absolutely thriving.

Even so, the secular world consistently mischaracterizes Jesus and his followers, as hypocritical, judgy, Jesus freaks; shutting down at the mention of his name and conflating extremists with his followers. At times, rightly so.

Compare that to back in the day, when people couldn't get enough of Jesus and were thirsting for him, his healing, mobbing him, following him around, skipping meals, to sit and listen to him all day, and straining to touch even the "hem of his garment."

He hasn't changed, nor has the need of or value of what he offers, however, the perception of him has.

Love

We thrive, when we feel loved and when love is a verb. We get creative and talkative and serene and chuckle unselfconsciously, when we feel seen and accepted.

> *"...you are precious to me. You are honored, and I love you." Isaiah 43:4*

However, the time spent focusing on how cherished and adored we actually are, is usually pretty brief. This part quickly blurs past, like a filmstrip going at hyperspeed. In some church circles, the "goal" appears to instead focus more on what is wrong with us.

While Jesus spoke frequently of love, he also embodied it. When he met a woman "caught" in the act of adultery (were these townsmen spying through her window or listening with a cup to the wall?) he pulled up next to her and talked, when he wasn't "supposed" to; not to a woman. He was relational. He wasn't doing drive by directives. He told her he didn't condemn (criticize or judge) her. And yes, there is more to this verse, but for now, for the sake of this discussion, pause on the "no condemning" part.

Meanwhile, these townsmen wanted to *murder* this woman, for what she'd been doing.

Somehow though, the Jesus of today, gets associated with the nefarious attitudes of the townsmen back then. This couldn't be a bigger lie. He actually said the exact opposite of what the woman was expecting to hear; the cultural norm of that time period. Expecting to die, she felt loved, instead.

If we just spend time fixating on how to love people in a manner that they will actually feel it, know it, believe it, experience it, it's possible . . . God has the capacity to do the rest.

At times we resort to lecturing or announcing we don't condone a behavior. This tends to show up, when addressing gay people.

My challenge to anyone reading this, is to spend more time on the love part and to just hang there, for (5) minutes, (5) hours, (5) days, (5) years. Build a relationship. And only after that, examine if it's imperative, to announce to that friend, you don't condone their lifestyle.

The changing of another person's heart isn't part of our assignment or concern. Humans, for the most part, do not like being told what to do, who to be, how to be, or how to feel. This is not our job. We have our hands full, in getting ourselves in order.

"...work out your own salvation with fear and trembling."
Philipans 2:12

When clients choose to come in to my office, they are inviting me in to their process. If I were to walk the streets approaching people and telling them to change or offering unsolicited advice, this would not go well. By the time they voluntarily come to me, their hearts are already prepared.

* * *

Now, as for freedom, this can be many things.

Freedom Of Finance

When Jesus regularly endorsed freedom, it's certainly possibile he was also referring to financial freedom. Financial hardship is one of the most oppressive struggles on earth. Financial hardship drives us to make desperate decisions and sometimes these decisions enslave us even further.

In addition, finances impact our relationships. Finances are the number (5) reason for divorce, according to the National Library of Medicine, cited at 37% as of April 2023.

The Bible endorses financial wisdom. Deuteronomy 28:12-13 announces you will be lenders, not borrowers. And later, Proverbs 22 discouragingly points out, the borrower is a servant to the lender. Additionally, Ecclesiastes 11:2 advises us to diversify investments.

In *Rich Dad Poor Dad* (1997), author Robert Kiyosaki recommends making money work for you. . .24 hours a day, like little ($) employees. He advises this versus working *for* money, and as a slave *to* money, as the way to financial freedom. He calls this financial literacy. He repeatedly makes the point to use the greatest natural and free resource we have to do this; our minds.

When it comes to money and the church, the model is often: church leaders accumulate and parishioners contribute, sometimes to their own detriment. It's possible parishioners can do a lot more with their money to help further God's kingdom, if it's invested and accruing.

The approach to money seems to be, just let it be and hope for the best, essentially avoidant. It's as if to focus on money for more than a brief moment, is not moral.

Becoming wise as a serpent, could mean getting as prepared and informed as humanly possible. This could mean identifying legal strategies offered by financial planners and tax specialists. However, this appears to be interpreted as a way *not* to trust God. Even seeing a therapist has been interpreted, in this manner.

A retired pastor I know, shared with me that he did not learn financial literacy growing up. It wasn't part of his church culture nor his family culture. He prayed for things to get better. He worked harder for the dollar, for survival, to provide for his family, and regularly tithed.

However, the lesson of making the dollar work for him, instead, such as through passive income, asset accumulation, and royalty income, was not part of his childhood or church's culture. As a result, he just ignored learning money.

In contrast, there is a training team of Christian entrepreneurs, investors, and millionaires, currently touring the US. They are training in financial literacy as a means to an end, not as the end goal. The philosophy is to get into financially free and capable positions to come to the aid of large groups of others in need, be changemakers, and use money, in the way it was intended, as a servicing tool.

Emotional Freedom

Another component of freedom is emotional freedom. Fear of people, people pleasing, and anxiety frequently ripple through the church. The Bible again and again reminds believers not to fear people.

" . . . so I will have no fear. What can mere people do to me?"
Hebrews 13:6

Jesus also role modeled a confident authority that caused people's jaws to drop and to fall into silence. He demonstrated this mentality through a variety of responses and behaviors. In John 5:41 he states

"Your approval means nothing to me."

This Jesus was not apologetic.

Being aware of Jesus' behavior and quoting Bible verses doesn't necessarily change the above mentioned tendencies, miraculously or overnight.

Fortunately, the availability of research and help through various channels, is plentiful and overflowing, in today's world. For example, a support group can be accessed by the click of a mousepad, on a Zoom call. A podcast from a licensed professional can be accessed for free on social media platforms.

Mental health and overall well-being-assistance have never been such a part of the cultural conversation and so accessible. While God can directly and supernaturally drop a miracle into your lap, while you are alone in your room, there are many other ways to access the gifts he has in store for you.

Prayers can illuminate blessings, stimulate epiphanies, and point toward sources of healing. Reaching out to a resource, doing research, or visiting a church, are some ways of starting to take action to tap into the available options.

As in James 4:8

"Come close to God and he will come close to you..."

Some have described to me, the struggle to take that first step, make that phone call, send that first text. Sometimes that hesitation lasts for years. Sometimes people just aren't ready. And sometimes people regret hesitating for so long. What it will take for your emotional freedom will require self examination and perseverance. It will require you taking ownership for your healing. We will get more in depth on activation steps in the next chapters. Briefly stated, this could be setting boundaries, when you are tired. It could be getting help with a troubling relationship. It could be exercising every day. This could mean leaving an oppressive job.

In the book *Relentless: From Good to Great to Unstoppable* (Grover, 2014) the author describes how athletes would fly out to his elite Chicago compound to talk about their personal mission statement, to workout, to get challenged, and to sort out a shortcoming or court performance problem. Sometimes these athletes were Kobe Bryant or Michael Jordan. Sometimes they flew out to his facility, immediately following a game.

The level of talent or knowledge is irrelevant. We all need assistance, coaches, advisors, mentors, a team of people, throughout various parts of our lives. God intended us for connection and community. He's gifted us all with a different range of talent and knowledge, wherein, we can greatly complement one another in areas in which we lack or have blind spots.

Critical Assessment

Examine what, if anything, is impeding you from activating change, right now. Examine what internal narratives may be running the show on autopilot.

If you are tethered to a past that haunts and holds you captive, then it might be time to seek out wise counsel, to help set you as free as Jesus intended, all along.

Freedom Through Discipline

Jocko Willinck wrote a book called *Discipline Equals Freedom: Field Manual Mk1-MOD1* (2020). Through relentless discipline, he achieved what many consider a highly desired position; he became a Navy Seal. He has parlayed that into his own podcast, being an author, a featured guest, and an interviewee on numerous platforms.

Discipline can be likened to self control and patience, both fruits of the spirit. Once again, traits that can lead us to our best lives. As Proverbs tells us

> *" . . . better to have self-control than to conquer a city." Proverbs 16:32*

Many highly successful business and entertainment industry professionals endorse sobriety and attribute this disciplined choice to aiding in their success.

Freedom through discipline can lead to prosperity.

The option to exercise total freedom in drinking, eating, and doing anything at any time, are all options available to the believer. But the data indicates, this is not the path to maintaining freedom. And as 1Peter 1:13 states

> *"So think clearly and exercise self control . . ."*

The irony, however, is to do anything and everything we want at any moment, easily results in captivity all over again. This could look like addiction, contracting an STD, or draining a savings account.

When Paul writes in 1 Corinthians 10:23 and 1 Corinthians 6:12

> *"All things are possible, but not all things are profitable"* and *". . . even though I am allowed to do anything, I must not become a slave to anything."*

Perhaps he mentions these, intending to also protect our freedom.

Physical Freedom

We have the right to bodily autonomy, consent, and protection. We have the right to say "no" and to decide who and when to let others physically close. While Chapter 6 goes into a full discussion of emotional and verbal boundaries, this section points out that physical boundaries, for our physical freedom, are also integral. Tremendous trauma has occurred due to bodily violations.

Unhealed and untreated, the echoes from physical violations can be carried in to our adult relationships, our churches, and on to our children. In short, hurt people hurt people. Perhaps we determine never to be violated in the same way, and the bullied becomes the bully. Or boundaries were completely ignored growing up and we, therefore, have blindspots, where boundaries should be. Whether victimizer or victimized, it is imperative to address this wounding. It will not *just go away*.

We are only as sick as our secrets. The cycle of physical and sexual violation must stop with us, if and when we identify it, regardless of our level of participation. Whether you've been exploited or re enacted, I recommend getting assistance, right away, and talking to a therapist. You are never too far in or too far gone. This is a lie. This topic is often shrouded in shame and can be very difficult to identify and address. We are never too broken, to address our struggles and heal.

Freedom is also currently being stolen from people, by enslaving them, here in this country, through labor and sex trafficking. Frequently, the most vulnerable, children, are targeted. The United States is the biggest consumer of compelled, coerced children, into sexual servitude, according to the *World Population Review* (2023). California is at the top of the list and San Diego is a hotbed. However we got here, we are here.

Jesus sharply warns against the harm of children, in Luke 17:2 and states

> *"It would be better to be thrown into the sea with a millstone hung around your neck than to cause one of these little ones to fall into sin."*

For the God-given right of physical freedom to be experienced by all and captives to be set free, we need to be the hands and feet of God; we need to help one another. Enslaved children need rescuing. By healthy adults. The little ones literally cannot do this alone. However, if the adults are not shored up on their own physical or sexual trauma, nor crystal clear on what boundaries belong where, how will they be effective?

There are herculean efforts, currently, at play, to mitigate change. However, they seem like drops in the ocean. Here in San Diego, Point Loma Nazarene University is a major research hub for human trafficking. North County Lifeline is an active ally, as well. The men who put together "The Sound of Freedom" movie from Operation Underground Railroad are certainly effectuating their powerful purpose in saving kids. Their mantra is "God's children are not for sale."

In Psalm 139:13

> *"You made all the delicate, inner parts of my body and knit me together in my mother's womb."*

Each of us is individually cherished by God and deserves physical freedom, as well.

Power

Jesus also repeatedly reminded his people of our power, authority, and strength. And in Proverbs believers are called *Lions*.

Credit: Marie Currie via MarieCurrie1@gmail.com

Fearing man is anathema to Jesus' whole healed identity he planned for us. In Philipians 1:28

> *"Don't be intimidated in any way by your enemies. This will be a sign to them that they are going to be destroyed, but that you are going to be saved, even by God himself."*

Remember how Jesus encouraged and empowered his followers.

In Luke 10:19 he states

> *"Look, I have given you authority over all the power of the enemy, and you can walk among snakes and scorpions and crush them. . ."*

He would know. Even when captured, in the face of his murderers and torturers, he continued composed and in control.

> *"...If I said anything wrong, you must prove it. But if I'm speaking the truth, why are you beating me?" John 18:23*

He demonstrated such healthy detachment and independence of thought and action, those who hated him could not handle it. They were spiraling, literally spitting on him, at a complete loss of self control, run by their emotions.

Operating from what appears to be their limbic systems, they opted to release a criminal into society, in exchange for killing Jesus; who healed, loved, and stood up to them.

Examining Jesus and his followers through this lens of power doesn't get the gravitas other verses do. For example, in some churches, being more like a doormat gets conflated with being Christ like. Those painted and carved depictions of Jesus seem to be impacting not just the outside world.

Agency

Agency is a psychological concept of self efficacy. Jesus possessed this in spades. Another term for this that could easily be applied is self sovereignty. Jesus demonstrated this in John 10:18 with

> *"No one can take my life from me. I sacrifice it voluntarily."*

He demonstrated his free will and non pressured compliance. If you'll notice, he did not speak with powerless "You won't let me's" or "Let me see if I can's." No permission requested.

Part of agency is owning it. Being accountable for oneself and all that entails, rather than offloading this responsibility onto someone else and expecting them to make it better. When we are not fully accountable for our words and actions and blame others for things like our angry reactions, we give our power over to them; to press our buttons, pull the strings, or ruin our day.

However, when that power is turned over to God *and we* find ways to make it better, we can return to the healthiest version of ourselves; thriving and free. We can then engage relationships, not as hostages to another's reactions, but rather fully operational as we were intended.

Remember

> *"For God did not give us a spirit of fear and timidity, but of power, love, and self discipline."* 2 Timothy 1:7

In addition, words like "I might/sort of/maybe/possibly" refer to the *probability* of an action, rather than the *activation* of it. There is no agency or sovereignty there.

In the present day church community lexicon, there appears to be a challenge in stating *I don't want to.* As if the expression of want or not to want is wrong.

To only operate in emotion and want is unbalanced and so is operating in denial of want, by operating only in logic. I suggest living in the in between of neither extremely emotional nor extremely cerebral. How to achieve being in-between or centered will be addressed in Chapter 7.

The nuance of the in between, takes a lot more work. It isn't the short hand of "I'll just never do that " or "I'll just always do this." It can take extra care and time. Sometimes, it requires a case by case evaluation of what's best in that given moment. Looking at your time availability, energy, promises to your family, frustration levels, finances, nourishment, exercise, may help with navigating the in betweens.

To lock out *ever* saying "I don't want to" believing church goers are called to *always* say "yes" to ministry, no matter how you feel, could lead to some exhaustion, resentment, and potentially harmful situations.

Part of agency is owning your word and what you've committed to. This could mean following through, finding a replacement, cancelling, or letting someone know you'll be late. In some church environments, the rules of thoughtfulness seem to go out the window.

Freedom Inside

Incredible survivors, like Viktor E. Frankl, really grasped the weight of these concepts. He survived (4) concentration camps. He places quite a high value on freedom in between stimulus and response in his book *Man's Search for Meaning* (Frankl, 1946). Nelson Mandela, while locked up, focused on not allowing his spirit to be demoralized. Freedom internalized, for both of these men, was like oxygen, to put it mildly.

Credit: Mary Taylor via Pexels.com

Imagine embracing your God given freedom, agency, authority, power, and actionable love. Imagine relinquishing disempowered or fearful representations of being a follower of Christ.

"Such love has no fear, because perfect love expels all fear. If we are afraid, it is for fear of punishment, and this shows that we have not fully experienced his perfect love." 1 John 4:18

Credit: Katerina Holmes via Pexels.com

CHAPTER 6: EXECUTION

> *"Thank you for making me so wonderfully complex! Your workmanship is marvelous - how well I know it." Psalm 129:14*

Our true identity, is majestically designed by God, to be conquerors, powerful, like lions, treading on serpents and scorpions, fearing no man, disregarding religious bloviating, and free.

Choose To Renew Your Mind

However, to read this, know this, believe this, and live in this is another thing. The battle rages mightily in the mind. Thoughts left unattended can seem to have an agenda of their own. According to cognitive behavioral theory, thoughts impact emotions and emotions impact what comes out of our mouths and how we behave. Noticing and addressing thoughts, or allowing them to pass through, without getting hung up on one particular idea can be quite freeing.

At other times, the job at hand might be to stop them, replace them, or calm them. To be armed with the recognition that this task will arise from time to time, can be a quite useful and proactive strategy. Those that think this is a one and done or even an indicator of some sort of personal failure, will struggle more.

Left to it's own devices, the brain "drifts toward entropy" according to Michael Ckiszentmihalyi (2009) of *Flow: The Psychology of Optimal Experience*. Redirecting this drift can be a regular and persistent pursuit. Part of our daily maintenance is mind maintenance.

Think of daily requirements for optimal well being. They include all the recommendations our doctors have been saying since time immemorial. To exist we need oxygen, food, water, and sleep. However, to live longer and more robustly, doctors recommend we sleep (8) hours a night, exercise regularly (a minimum of 150 minutes a week), eliminate smoking, and keep alcohol intake to a few drinks a week. We are also encouraged to get Vitamin D from the sun and to connect with one another, in a meaningful way.

Think of mental maintenance as essential for optimal thriving. Without a daily practice you won't perish, but you certainly won't be your best. Just as, without connecting with another person, you'll still be alive, but the color and the quality of existence may fall flat. If you don't exercise, you may still wake up tomorrow, but the benefits of an exercise induced serotonin boost won't be present. The benefits to your heart and joints won't be realized and a whole host of complications may arise.

Chosen Perspective

Often, events occurring around us are neutral and we assign a value to them or personalize them. If someone cuts us off in traffic we may interpret this as a direct affront to our personhood. We may feel targeted or attribute ourselves to always getting the short end of the stick. We channel the interpretation of events through our personal lens, including our worldview, how we were raised, our values, and our views of ourselves.

In reality, there is a lot of negativity and in reality that car did cut you off. However, to regularly funnel occurrences through the lens of being unlucky, or as the one who always gets the short end the stick, will negatively affect your mood. How you choose to view these instances will dramatically impact your feelings about them.

Brain Plasticity

A scientific discovery that is incredibly encouraging is that of brain plasticity. The concept of brain or neuro plasticity states that we have the capacity to restructure the shapes of our brains and re circuit our neuropathways. A reason why this is tremendous, is that formerly forgone conclusions about our mental pathways, due to factors, such as our upbringing, are no longer. Our destiny, so to speak, is not set in stone. We have more agency than we ever thought possible.

If you imagine your repetitive thoughts circling over a particular concept or memory as a needle in a well worn groove of a record and that we can move the needle into a new path and establish a new well worn groove, this is a way to view neuroplasticity. Just because your brain tends to slip over into a well worn path, does not mean you are stuck or trapped like that. With awareness, implementation, and rehearsal, you can strengthen and deepen the groove of something different.

Gratefulness

Gratefulness exercises are a way to harness your thoughts and boost your mood. Doing so shows surges in dopamine and seratonin, boosts happiness, boosts energy, and provides health benefits, such as combatting immunity suppression.

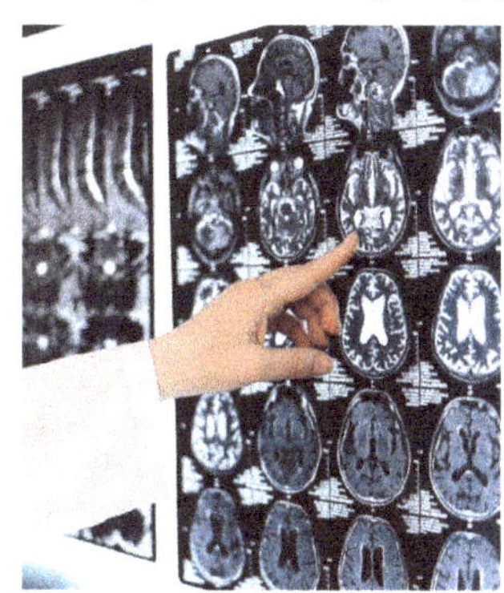

Credit: Anna Shvets via Pexels.com

In 2017, a study by Kyeong, et al., used an fMRI scan (functional Magnetic Resonance Imaging), which identifies blood flow to a brain area, as an area in use. This study found correlations between gratitude, the amygdala, and emotional regulation.

Complementary to this research, the Bible states

> *". . . whatever is true, whatever is worthy of respect, whatever is just, whatever is pure, whatever is lovely, whatever is commendable, if something is excellent or praiseworthy, think about these things." Phil 4:8*

Interestingly, this verse has biological benefits for us. One way to look at this verse, is to examine the good in your life, what is working, what is going well, and what is going right. This is not a power of positive thinking exercise, such as, "I am the most beautiful successful intelligent being on the planet." Instead, this is sifting through the internal noise and excavating some facts, telling yourself the *truth* about yourself and your accomplishments.

We do have a choice where to place our focus. And where we focus, our energy goes. We also have a finite amount of energy, so discerning where to expend it, matters.

Be careful about directing mistakes into negative narratives about oneself and non deserving self talk. Ironically, we are likely to give God the glory for the good, but perseverate over our missteps.

Critical Assessment Action

Take a look at (5) alternative interpretations of the event at hand.

Are there any other reasons, any at all, that could have led that car to cut off your car, in traffic?

When the Bible recommends we meditate, there are biological bonuses, as well. Research reveals meditators have thicker prefrontal cortexes, the rational area of the brain; Another example of brain plasticity. So meditators might be less led around by emotional chaos. When God says he is not the God of confusion, perhaps this is a path he's provided to allow us clarity.

As mentioned earlier, a practice is a method of mental maintenance. I recommend a daily practice, which can be a variety of tools. Finding the most effective combination for yourself is a bit of an expedition. An activity I recommend for clients is to take moments in the morning, before even opening your eyes, before the day has begun. Be intentional about setting the tone. Before the tone of falling behind or racing around or before worry about an upcoming meeting has set in. Establish (3) things to be grateful for. Look for fresh impactful moments from the past (24) hours and take some time to absorb them. This is a way to re train your brain and maximize it's plasticity.

Boundaries

Boundaries are fundamental to every therapist's playbook and in the New Testament "let your yes be yes and your no be no" is the most straightforward definition of boundaries there is. Later, in 2 Corinthians 1:17-19 Paul asks

> *"Do you think I am like people of the world who say 'Yes' when they really mean 'No'?...our word to you does not waver between 'yes' and 'no.' For Jesus Christ the Son of God does not waver between 'Yes' and 'No.' ... as God's ultimate YES he always does what he says."*

In some arenas of Biblical teaching, saying "no" only went as far as premarital sex and drugs. However, this leaves out a richly textured landscape of emotional, spiritual, and additional physical boundaries. In learning the entirety of boundaries, self efficacy, free will, and healthy relationships can emerge.

Critical Assessment

Take a moment to consider this potential disparity, in your own experience of boundary development. In what areas do you struggle to set boundaries, if any?

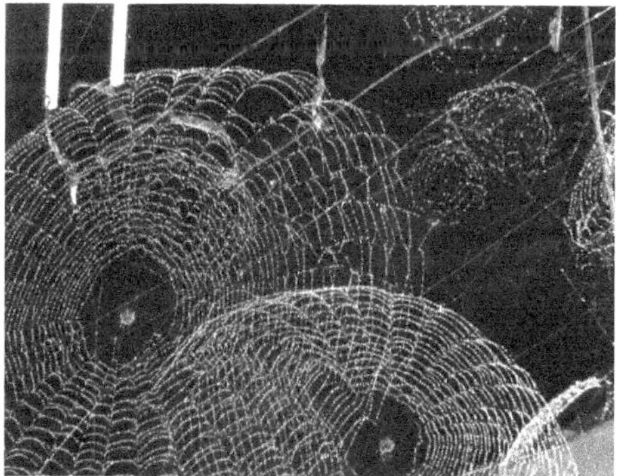

Credit: Marie Currie via MarieCurrie1@gmail.com

Without them, the ensuing entanglements might end up looking like spider webs.

The Gatekeeper

You are the gatekeeper and your best lifelong advocate. You are the one who puts your head on your pillow each night and sleeps with your thoughts. You will always be the common factor in every job and relationship you invite in to your life. No one else is going to do this for you as consistently and precisely as you. Not the church, the job, nor your significant other.

Credit: Marie Currie via MarieCurrie1@gmail.com

It's *you*. Ask God for the discernment and strength on implementation and maintenance. This may show up in the form of like-minded individuals or an unexpected opportunity, along the way.

Understandably, "no" can often be very difficult, as it's often tightly intertwined with guilt. In Romans 14:22b it says

> *"Blessed are those who don't feel guilty for doing something they have decided is right."*

Implementing boundaries and then holding them can be very difficult with those who have been in your life for long periods of time. They know you a certain way and the majority won't like you changing the rules of long established roles, especially if you having little to no boundaries is benefitting them. It can be easier to set boundaries with new people, who may not know your old ways.

It can be scary. If you grew up in a household where there were no boundaries and people yelled or got violent when someone tried to set one or yours were ignored altogether, this may be part of the struggle.

Some people wait to set a boundary until they are ready to explode. Fearing their initial concern was too minute or petty, they save it, until it's a fiery inferno. However, saying it before it reaches that explosive level can reduce your blood pressure and preserve the relationship, if that is what you want. Find safe people with whom to start practicing small boundaries, today.

Credit: Duong Nhan via Pexels.com

Expect people not to like them. Also know, that a boundary does not cause a human being to disintegrate into powder, no matter how they insist it does. In fact, there will be those, that know, when they cry, you back down. There will be those that know, when they lash out, due to your boundary, you get scared and end up apologizing. If this holds you in check, this is like being a prisoner to the relationship.

Remember

> *"So you have not received a spirit that makes you fearful slaves...." Romans 8:15*

It's important to take ownership when you set a boundary. For example, state "I do not like this," versus telling the other person what is wrong with them and how they need to change. It's a chance for you to get clear on what you do and do not tolerate and then to *act*.

Hopefully the other person will get it and honor it, but it's more about you deciding when *you* will take action. If the other person does not like it, nor agree, it does not mean you are doing it "wrong." It could be helpful at that point to take the "yes and" approach with "I know you feel that way *and* nevertheless, my boundary remains."

At some point, it may be time to shake off dust and leave the reaction, that you are unable to control, to it's owner's responsibility.

To keep explaining and reminding the other person can be demoralizing. So can rationalizing and justifying the boundary. When we keep saying it over and over, but don't follow through, or explode and then give in, we teach the other person we don't mean it. Sure, we'll get fired up, but that other person understands the bottom line; they got their way. They may have had to endure you yelling, but their desired outcome occurred.

Within all of us is an adolescent testing and pushing

boundaries, trying to get away with it, this time, acutely aware of how many tries it takes to get the other to cave. Through a demonstration of *behavior*, either giving in or not, the lesson is learned and reinforced.

"What we can do is set limits on our own exposure to people who are behaving poorly; we can't change them or make them behave right." *Boundaries: When to Say Yes, How to Say No to Take Control of Your Life* (Townsend and Cloud, 2003).

Watching Jesus' example, with trifling questions, traps, and accusations, reveal that sometimes he chose not to respond. Nor did he step across the line to beg people to understand him. When we cross the line and over function for another person, this gives them permission to underfunction.

Jesus chose to address what was coming at him, on the occasions he deemed fit. He wasn't defensive or getting tangled up in the weeds of long involved explanations. He'd see the game for what it was.

Proactive Vs. Reactive

In the therapy world, this has been referred to as being proactive, rather than reactive. Jesus role modeled this beautifully. Getting to the place of choice rather than feeling pulled around by emotion is a cherished destination and a challenge for many.

In another instance

> *"'Teacher,' said an expert in religious law, you have insulted us, too, in what you just said. 'Yes' said Jesus...." Luke 11:45-46*

The displeasure from others did not launch him into fretting over trying to make everyone feel okay. His number one goal was definitely not to make sure everyone liked him or to ensure that no one ever had a hurt feeling.

While those used to being people pleased plotted his demise, he continued his agenda for setting captives free and healing people. He facilitated this by going off alone to pray and getting rest. He displayed *healthy detachment*.

He advised his followers to shake off dust, when unwelcome or not listened to, by disengaging. He was not about expending unnecessary energy, nor wasting his limited time on earth.

Credit: Ceejay Talam via Pexels.com

Critical Assessment

Imagine what it would be like to "shake off dust," and rather than pressing an issue, going and collecting yourself, through prayer, rest, writing, or talking to someone you trust. Strategize how you would concretely implement this and how you would handle the fallout.

Below, you'll find tools to check yourself, for the purpose of altering thought patterns. These are also a way of putting a name to common schools of thought. You aren't the only one.

Distortion #1 - Black And White Thinking

The antithesis of "yes, and" is the cognitive distortion of *black and white thinking*. It is also known as all-or- nothing thinking. Think of it as a teeter totter, wherein, when one side is good or up, the other side must be bad or down. There isn't room for nuance in the middle. It is a protective shorthand in reaching quick, often inaccurate judgments. It is a way of quickly closing the door of uncertainty or curiosity and more of a rigid way of thinking.

Distortion #2 - Emotional Reasoning

This can dip into *emotional reasoning*, another cognitive distortion. Remember when RadioHead sang just because you feel it, doesn't mean it's real? For example, feeling you are a hopeless case, you are stuck like this, that there is something innately wrong with you, does not mean it's true.

Breaking out of narratives like these must be a conscious choice; A conscious choice to challenge these thoughts, the moment you identify they are happening, with facts. For instance, if you made a mistake, challenge the feeling of hopelessness with the *fact* that you have the capacity to address the mistake and to equip yourself with more information, to improve, in the future.

Remind yourself of examples wherein you have, indeed, addressed previous mistakes and overcome. Reflect on these examples regularly.

Another way of viewing this is compassion for ourselves. The Bible tells us to love our neighbor *as we love ourselves.*

Well, what does this self love actually look and sound like?

I think it is in keeping our word to ourselves, such as, those moments, when we opt to get out of bed early and go work out, because we told ourselves we would. I think it is also honoring the still small voice within that is telling us something feels off or violating.

When we make our mistakes, it is talking to ourselves, (yes, we all talk to ourselves) in a proactive way, that promotes growth and solutions and change. Typically this is done with love and compassion, not angry judgment and impatient criticism.

Distortion #3 - Catastrophic Thinking

Another cognitive distortion that can become problematic, especially in regard to anxiety is *catastrophic thinking* looking at "what ifs" and extrapolating those out to a very fatalistic conclusion. It is no longer considered to be present in the here and now but instead detached from this moment and thinking out there and out there is full of uncontrollables. In combination with this type of thinking, tends to be a racing heart and shortness of breath.

One way of challenging this type of thinking is to ask yourself the likelihood of the catastrophe you are fearing, to actually occur. In addition, place a percentage on the possibility of this catastrophe. Lastly, look at what then. If indeed this catastrophe actually occurs, what then will you do? And then?

For further cognitive distortions, check into cognitive behavioral theory.

Credit: Anthony DeRosa via Pexels.com

CHAPTER 7: EMOTIONAL REGULATION

When we are in crisis, we tend to get myopic. Our scope of field and vision can narrow like a tunnel. Our options outside the tunnel, disappear into our blind spots, for awhile. We may forget our good qualities or the good qualities of our significant others. What we see and believe, in those moments can look, convincingly, very bleak. Having the capacity to self regulate and bring the entire field of vision back into our sightline, is a highly valuable skill to acquire.

When we are dysregulated, it is very difficult to problem solve. Think of this as the amygdala "hijacking" the prefrontal cortex, or going from the wise version of ourselves, to the 10 year old, driving the bus.

Breathing

This is one reason why breathing exercises are so highly recommended by a wide range of practitioners. Addressing the breathing first, can often radically change the trajectory of a person's physiological responses and rather quickly. It can also force the attention away from the predictions, to present bodily activity.

There is a built in relaxation mechanism that God has designed within our systems, called the vagus nerve. Deep intentional breathing can press this nerve and contribute to our calming down. This process can bring our attention back to attending to what is happening in the current moment, after breathing on autopilot day and night.

When we are present and centered, we are at our best.

Breathing exercises can be implemented in a variety of ways. Box breathing is just one method, as recommended in some military training. It is essentially imagining a box while inhaling, counting to (5), pausing at the imagined corner, and then exhaling, while imagining the additional side of the box, counting to (7), pausing at the next imagined corner, and then inhaling at the bottom of the box. The duration of the numbers while inhaling and exhaling are arbitrary. The point is to be slow and deliberate about your breathing and to extend the exhale longer than the inhale. The longer exhale stimulates the vagus nerve.

Sensorial

Adding in sensorial awareness of (3) sounds, (4) sensations, and (5) visuals, can help with centering and grounding. And by grounding, I mean being clear minded, rather than spiraling or racing thoughts. This exercise is literally redirecting your focus away from straying thoughts and instead placing them onto this present moment, through the awareness of each of your senses.

Take a moment right now, to tune in to any sounds to which you previously were not paying attention. Stop reading or scanning or planning your response to a text. Notice the car going by outside, or the birds chirping, or footsteps on the stairs. Repeat with all of your senses, throughout the day, when you catch your thoughts racing.

In some instances, physical sensations, like a hug, or your hand placed over your heart, can also be helpful. Therapist and author Anabel Gonzalez of *It's Not Me: Understanding Complex Trauma, Attachment, and Dissociation* (2018) references thinking of how you would calm and comfort a newborn or a puppy. It is a level of patience and gentleness, that often eludes us, when dealing with ourselves.

Scale

Another step toward getting grounded, is to utilize a scale of 1-10; with (10) being the most agitated you've ever been, and (1) being you are your best self. Pay attention, right now, to what your number is. Considering how you feel, right now, how close is this number to your ideal? Reflect on a time when your number was near (10) and what caused your number to climb or diminish. Attend to what number with which you communicate effectively and when you start losing it.

Orienting yourself through this number system can be helpful, during a disagreement or an uncomfortable staff meeting. Noticing your number escalation during these moments can inform you, that it might be time to start calming yourself back down, to your ideal number. Typically, we don't want to calm ourselves back down, when escalating. So using a number, instead, to be a guardrail, can be quite useful.

R. A. I. N.

Dr. Laurie Santos of the Happiness Lab podcast and Yale lecturer on the Science of Well Being suggests the acronym "R.A.I.N." originally developed by Michelle McDonald, senior mindfulness teacher. R: Recognize (observe and name what is going on) A: Accept (be with it, without changing it) I: Investigate with friendliness and N: Not identify (disentangle from the feelings, observing them coming and going).

Self Talk

Self talk makes a big difference in all of these exercises. Imagine what it is you've always needed to hear, when you get agitated. You may need to hear and know that it's going to be okay or that this moment will pass and is only temporary or that you only have (5) more minutes to endure this workout, or this conversation.

The tendency to use the opposite is quite common. We may push harder, to fix it, and attempt to force to make it better, to get out of discomfort quickly. We may also push others in these moments, in flailing efforts to get them to make it better for us. However, pushing and forcing are not the antidote. Taking your foot off the gas, is more likely to help.

Lecturing yourself that you are taking too long or are doing it wrong, does not tend to work, either. Not for long. Remind yourself this isn't "proof" that you are fatally flawed. Advocating this for yourself, internally, will help you advocate how you are spoken to, externally, also.

The strongest point for us emotionally is centered and present. This is where we make wiser decisions. We don't lash out as much and we don't tend to assume others responses are criticisms of flaws within our core. We don't get as hurt. In *There is Nothing Wrong with You: Going Beyond Self Hate* (1997) Cheri Huber discusses the internal mental battle we can have that wreaks havoc on our well being. She dissects how easy it is for us to argue a case against ourselves, determined to make ourselves just flat out wrong.

Think of an athlete's strongest position as lifting from the center, rather than off to the side, which could cause injury.

Credit: Erika Reyes via Pexels.com

Technology

In order to get extraordinarily clear to execute the above mentioned suggestions, it may be time to turn off the distractions. In *How to Break Up with Your Phone: The 30-Day Plan to Take Back Your Life* (2018) author Catherine Price recommends taking a sabbatical or a 24 hour detox from electronics, once a week.

The impacts on the nervous system, the attention span, and our moods are bearing out in the research. Since the smartphone release in 2011, feelings of uselessness and depression amongst teens have exploded, according to Jean Twenge of San Diego State University.

Credit: Roman Odintsov via Pexels.com

When designers work on a project, they can also see the data and psychological research on impacts on human beings. They can use it to suit their purposes, to captivate, or take captive our attention. Programming appears to be designed based on a variety of factors, including experiments and research, such as operant conditioning. In one such experiment, rats were given access to cocaine, not continuously, but intermittently. This appeared to produce a "subset of rats that display many of the core features of addiction, including escalation of drug intake, a binge-like pattern of drug-seeking . . .and high levels of drug seeking, during cue-induced reinstatement" (Garcia et al., 2020). The study demonstrates stimulation in the dorsomedial striatum (DMS) region of the brain, a critical player in addiction.

Knowing this, it stands to reason programmers would design

games and phones and all forms of entertainment in a similar and intermittent way, so as to stimulate the DMS and get the consumer into "binge-like" and "high levels of seeking" status.

And further, look at how you respond when a text comes in. Do you have a jolt or a forced decision each moment a text arrives? The automatic training that has been set up, to "text back, or else," is a set of expectations that many people have slipped into without question. Reports of increased anxiety have proliferated, surrounding technology, as well. Look at who is setting the rules for you, even on something as simple as returning a text.

Design implementation has a psychology behind it and knowing your own psychology and tendencies can be invaluable. Breaking the pattern may require "fasting" the technology and prayer. How can one actually be clear headed enough, to hear God's plan, if there is a never ending influx of technological stimuli?

Your mind my never be getting a break or a chance to recharge. Think of this principle like intermittent fasting, which theoretically gives the body a break from digesting food, providing a chance to reset and recover.

Credit: Cottonbro Studio via Pexels.com

CHAPTER 8: CONFLICT RESOLUTION

"Don't sin by letting anger control you, think about it over night..." Psalm 4:4

Jeremy's kids, Landon and Xavier, slowly unharnessed from their cramped seated positions in the back seat of the now sedentary vehicle. Both of them moved slower than usual, but their eye balls were alert and scanning. Jocelyn was also able to untether herself, reset an errant hair wisp back behind her left ear, and with her free hand open her door. She slid her high heeled feet out onto the gravel and the firmness of the ground felt certain to her and she appreciated this.

She slammed her front car door with a hearty snap of the hips, just like she'd learned in her kickboxing-for-mamas class, that's the power band! And she relished the resultant loud crashing sound of the door. She reached and unlatched the back door, sliding it open and melted a moment, seeing both children in uncertain and startled hesitation.

She motioned for both of them to come toward her and while hesitantly scooting up in his seat, Landon, the youngest, cleared his throat and with a wavery mini voice asked "Are you and daddy mad at us?"

* * *

How many of us got healthy role modeling on conflict resolution, growing up or on anger, for that matter? This is not an indictment on your family or upbringing, but more of a road map for insight, to track how you got here and how, if interested, you can choose another way to proceed.

You may be carrying around a method to manage disagreements and anger, that have been set in play at a very young age. These will show up in triggering situations, even at church. Remember the child development and brain discussion in chapter 3? It's possible this method is no longer serving you in your adult intimate partner relationships, or any relationships for that matter.

Credit: Angelo Martucci via Pexels.com

Consider the concept of the communication superhighway as the ultimate unimpeded pathway to being heard and understood. With this analogy, there are well documented methods that will shut down and block communication, fire up defensiveness, and choke the free flow of "traffic." If you resort to these tactics, you are guaranteed to damage your relationships. Sadly, these methods also regularly result in pushing the other person away, right when we need each other the most.

Conversely and most encouragingly, there are tried and true methods to make smooth, efficient, proceeding, even through challenging emotions and topics. If you use these methods, you will set yourself up with a better shot of actually accomplishing what you intend in a difficult conversation and you may establish an even stronger bond.

Road Blocks

Some common methods of handling conflict and anger include *bottle up and blast*. This is a method, that resorts to holding it all in for as long as stamina allows and then bursts forth with explosive intensity and often harsh words that will also need to be addressed later. The harsh words then become their own separate topic.

This method hopes the feelings will just go away or assumes initial concerns are too petty to address. There is also the fear of bringing concerns up, when things are good, fearing it will "ruin things" and fear of hurting the other's feelings. There is also fear of violent reprisal.

When these feelings do come billowing out, in all of their fury, they are typically accompanied by a sense of self righteous indignation and justification. After holding it in for so long and "just taking it" it's now time for the other person to get a piece of your mind or to get what they deserve. This method may also feel like pure survival protection.

Another common pattern is *conflict avoidance*. This is tip toeing around thorny topics, sometimes by being apologetic, overly accommodating, or acting like everything is fine. This tends to leave unresolved hot spots all over the place that could erupt at any moment. This is also known as pretending or brushing things under the rug.

Making nice, can be seen frequently at church. This is the version that seems to been conflated with loving Jesus; feel insulted or stomped on and just smile and say "Jesus loves you" or "Praise the Lord."

However, pretending is not a value endorsed by Jesus. A horrible alternative is to take it out on family, sometimes in secret. This would be the "blast" portion of the withheld anger. If it seems it is more acceptable to blast one's family, rather than those at church, recheck this presumption. It isn't. Blasting either is unacceptable.

Ephesians 4:26 tells us to be angry without sinning. Anger is an emotion that indicates something is awry. It's in us for a reason. The key is in how we manage it. Using your words, rather than your actions, when angry, is one way to deflate it. Specifically, name the anger and own it, rather than slamming doors, expecting others to get it.

People have described to me, going from 0 - 100 without knowing how they got there; they suddenly . . . are just there. This is the part that requires you to learn yourself. Frequently, this requires help, as changing this pattern is no easy task.

To unleash at 100, often means people have crossed the "I don't care what I say" line or worse, the "I don't care what I do" line, as coined by Dr. Adams in *The Choices Program: How to Stop Hurting the People Who Love You* (2016) book. This lack of self control damages people and relationships.

These behaviors are learned and can therefore, be unlearned, no matter what upbringing, role modeling, or victimization you endured. People don't tend to come out of the womb defensive and lashing out.

New behaviors can replace these old behaviors, instead. The mindset that this is just how you are and will always be, is just patently untrue. You are not powerless to your past. Resist the urge to swallow any untrue narrative about your capabilities. Perhaps this is what Ephesians 4 refers to in putting off the old self and taking on the new.

If you are involved in relational violence of any kind, it's time to stop, set up a safety plan, and get help.

Fair Fighting

This concept is not typically the first idea that comes to mind, when people imagine conflict. Conflict averse people tend to have reasons for this. Conflict, growing up was potentially scary and dangerous. Most people I interview take the word "conflict" and extrapolate that into something extreme. This appears to lead to a strong aversion to conflict and conflict avoidant behaviors. However, conflict does not have to be scary or violent or never ending.

To keep avoiding conflict and only getting in to it, when it's explosive and out of control, is reinforcing an unhealthy cycle of conflict. Which is to avoid it, because it tends to be horrible, and in so avoiding, it explodes unexpectedly and tends to be horrible.

In addition, intimate partners tend to fight at 11:00pm, when they are tired. Alcohol can also be a factor in escalating the conflict into something it doesn't need to be. Put another way, *people tend to fight, when they are at their worst and firing on only a few cylinders.* This is a setup for failure.

Without boundaries and containment around conflict, things like coming home from work can become a landmine to be avoided at all costs. Unresolved arguments can be felt even before setting foot through the front door. Subsequently, unresolved conflict can lead to being followed around the house, room to room. This can lead to the fight that is never ending, that will keep morphing into something even worse.

In stark contrast, *fair fighting* involves neither fleeing, following, nor viciously engaging. It involves learning skills many did not get growing up and unlearning other unhelpful methods. It is powerful to have this insight, as it can make room to learn, right now.

Operating in what is, rather than what is "supposed" to be, can be tremendously helpful. The bar of expectation for another can often be put upon a person that doesn't want it. In therapy school, I was taught "you can't take people to Paris, if they only want to cross the street."

Accepting the reality of where you are at and the other person is at, can reduce unnecessary attempts to push or force a situation. Controlling that person or situation is an illusion. So start with setting yourself free, by telling yourself the truth.

One way of opening the channel is acknowledging the other person. We all have the need to be seen and heard. Acknowledgment is not collusion or agreement. It is seeing from the other person's point of view and extending understanding for how they arrived there. You may still simultaneously disagree with the outcome and may still need to address an injury. It is again, the concept of "yes, and" rather than either or. One person does not need to be painted as all bad or all wrong to have harmed you. The injured party isn't all saintly or all in the right, either. Disregarding who is "right" and who is "wrong" and seeking solutions together can be a much more fruitful endeavor.

De escalating methods can include taking turns, setting time limits on thorny topics, taking responsibility for one's own thoughts and feelings, abandoning name calling, labeling, and yelling.

In addition, choose to stick to (1) area of concern at a time. The brain can only handle so much at once. Think of setting you and your significant other up for success, by keeping an eye on information overload. This is also known as "kitchen sinking" (throwing everything in but the kitchen sink).

If there is escalation during a conflict, take breaks when necessary and return to re engage, when regulated, and safe. Communicate ahead of time that you will be doing this.

John Gottman in *The seven Principles for Making Marriage Work* (1999) discusses the concept of the "Four Horseman of the Apocalypse" in relationships. Through his seminal work, researching couples in a lab, studying conflict styles and pulse rates, among other variables, he came up with an accurate prediction of divorce, within three minutes of observation, 96% of the time.

He distilled down the most toxic variables to contempt, criticism, defensiveness, and stonewalling. He categorizes criticism as "diagnosing a partner's personality defects," and then waiting to be thanked. He describes defensiveness or "warding off a perceived attack," through counterattacking. Think of contempt as coming from a perceived superior place, looking down on the other. He suggests this can show up in correcting a partner's grammar, during an argument. Contempt is correlated with troubling immune system functioning, which can open a doorway to infectious diseases. Stonewalling is essentially shutting down and shutting the other person out.

If we know with scientific certainty what dooms marriages to failure, it stands to reason, the polar opposite, might save them. Those who tend toward marital "mastery" per Gottman, are those who take suggestions in stride with "that's interesting, tell me more. How am I contributing to this?" This is just one example, which happens to be the antithesis of defensiveness.

Differences of opinion should never escalate to violence, on another person, animal, or object. If this is what you grew up with and you are conflict avoidant, no wonder. But these are not the rules or determinants for your destiny.

You are the one, now, to set new standards and redefine your relationships. You do not have to repeat what you learned or act out, because you weren't shown a healthier way, growing up. Give yourself the authority to decide to do things differently. Our differences of opinion do not have to be threatening and can be incredible opportunities for us to learn and grow. Learning a new way, is on us all, as we "adult."

> *"For we are each responsible for our own conduct." Galatians 6:5*

Credit: Emrecan Algul via Pexels

CHAPTER 8.5: CONFLICT RESOLUTION PART 2

Feedback

Providing and receiving feedback can be a sensitive area. Proverbs repeatedly refers to a hallmark of wisdom that is the ability to take feedback. Surrounding oneself with wise counsel, can be invaluable. Our teams can include mentors, coaches, pastors, therapists, financial advisors, mediators, attorneys, and specialists. We are not subject matter experts on all things. We are surrounded by a world of expertise. Why not tap into it?

Also, keep in mind, the discussion on all-or-nothing thinking. Stay away from accepting opinions from all those who want to give it or divulging to all who demand it. There may be many. Resist the urge to shut everyone down, as well. Find the best middle, for you.

Be selective and exercise wisdom in dispensing feedback, as well, whether it's as a parent, a spouse, or a supervisor.

Delineating between *evaluative* and *objective* feedback is priceless. Sometimes feedback gets confused with being honest or used as an excuse to let it rip. On the flip side of the same coin of this logic, is "people are too sensitive and I'm not going to walk on eggshells."

Evaluative feedback can make people feel judged or defensive. It usually gives people the impression their core value is under scrutiny. For example, evaluative feedback tends to involve labeling and would call an offending person names, such as "You hurt me, because you are just an (x,y,z)." If feedback gives any impression of "there is something wrong with you" it will often turn it into a race toward who can point out the most flaws in the other. These can appear like two year olds swatting at each other.

However, objective feedback looks more at behaviors and concrete things that *can* be changed, without merging this with the core worth of the person. People tend to stay open longer, when feedback is given objectively, devoid of emotional attack. Objective feedback for the offending party should be specific and direct. "I was affected in this (specific) way by your (specific) behavior, and I would like this (specific) instead."

When feedback is given in vague, general, flowery terms, it is hard to follow. It's more vulnerable and scary to be specific. This can be the most effective clean shot toward resolution. Do not engage this method, if there is any violence in this relationship.

The Pause

Additionally, taking the pause can be incredibly powerful and can completely change the game. If you feel compulsively ready to fire back a text, for example, and it feels like it must immediately burst forth from your fingertips, do not send it. *Take the pause.* Additionally, pay attention to how long it takes for you to calm down and work with your biology to get there.

Recall times when you've said or texted something you regret. How long did it take for you to regret it and even come up with something else to say, instead, or in some cases realize you did not need to say anything at all. Sometimes this can mean telling the other person you need a break and that *you'll be back* if safe to do so. Use the time to calm down and then, do as you said you would and come back.

Apologizing

When apologizing, applying the principles laid out previously in this chapter, will come in handy.

These include seeing from the other person's perspective and acknowledging the harm they must have suffered, as a result. According to Gottman, the quality of the friendship makes an impact on the repair, as well. In addition, be succinct and direct. Take responsibility clearly for your part. Don't muddy the waters with how the other person is also responsible or with how you were raised. In treatment groups with violent offenders, whether on an aircraft carrier or in a 52-week anger management class, a barrier to progress, I observed, was blaming the partner for "causing" the anger which "justified" a physical outburst.

In addition, provide a real strategy to prevent this same mistake from repeating. Don't use platitudes or martyrdom. "Well, I'll just never be friends with anyone of the opposite sex, again."

Apologizing does not include demanding forgiveness. Nor does it include demanding the other person get over it, as you "said sorry." More specifically, an apology is not a transactional demand.

Taking a peek under the hood for this information could be useful to see what needs altering, not to dwell there in perpetual blame, guilt, or shame spirals. This isn't a recommendation to just immerse in all the wrongs you've ever committed or suffered. If there are blindspots you uncover, address these blindspots, now. Be proactive with action steps toward healing and resolution.

The Recipient Of The Apology

Forgiveness is endorsed Biblically and it is also important to keep applying the principles discussed within the pages of this book. We know God gives us instructions in our best interests. Over and over we see biological and emotional advantages to following his instructions. Over and over we see his design is intended toward our ultimate wellness and wholeness and yes, freedom. As discussed in previous pages, freedom can include emotional freedom.

However, forgiving and accepting the apology, before you are ready, is not healthy, and is not freedom. Remember to be your own gatekeeper, and be wise as a serpent, as you protect and search your own heart. Examine your motives. Don't rush over your own experience of injury, to forgive, relieve the tension, and give the other person satisfaction, without your own. Can you see a way forward in this relationship, as a result of the apology and the solution offered for change?

On the other end of the spectrum, holding an apology hostage and nursing your hurt, is ultimately embittering yourself. Keep applying the principles of "yes and." Take the time to sort this through, neither rushing, closing off, or extending something you don't really believe.

It might take awhile to unlearn some long held habits, but starting now is a day sooner than tomorrow. None of us know what will happen tomorrow. Starting on something, even the smallest piece, now, and chiseling away each day, will add up. Whereas, waiting until you are motivated to make huge changes may feel too overwhelming to even begin.

Let today be the day you start to take ownership for your words and behaviors, nothing more, nothing less. Let today be the day you stop allowing anyone to hold your past over your head and you emotionally hostage. Let today be the day you start getting free.

Another option for assistance is marriage counseling, wherein, marriage counselors can intervene and teach conflict resolution skills, in the moment, in real time.

Credit: Benjamin Farren via Pexels.com

CHAPTER 9: AGENTS OF CHANGE

What causes people to activate and actually turn the corner after saying "I want to get out of this relationship, lose weight, start working out, get up earlier, start my own business, cut down on drinking" and what leaves the others drinking more, eating more, sleeping in later . . . instead? In therapy school, we learn people don't change, until they are in enough pain.

Detailed throughout this chapter are some real life interviews and examples, that may spur you forward, before the pain gets too great. Interestingly, what tends to happen when great change is effectuated, people want to give it away to someone else. They often become agents of change.

Gretchen Lindner certainly did so, losing 80 lbs between 2019 and 2021 after 20 years of repeated frustrating attempts. And she did it *during* COVID. Not only has she transformed, shedding the weight, she coaches others in how to do it like she did. She's living it *and* paying it forward.

She felt the flickers of actual change when she began to tell herself "It's not an option any more; this is possible. This is doable. You can do this. The people before me were able to do this; they did it. I can do this, too. Tammy, someone I know, did it."

Previous destructive thoughts that would completely derail her efforts would be "You're done. It's in your genes."

Plus she augmented her success trajectory with the following steps:

1. She had support. She had a trusted accountability partner who'd succeeded first and Gretchen knew she wouldn't be left behind or judged in her efforts or lack therein.

2. She has a community of ongoing support throughout her continuing process.

3. She continues to grow through education and supplementary reading.

4. She coaches and encourages others. She gives back.

Gretchen observes the change versus a lack of change in the students she coaches, noting the attitude of "throwing a credit card at the next solution" and notes "those who don't engage in community aren't successful." She's sees those "who are excited to tell me what they are learning . . .engaging" in the learning materials, voluntarily, outside class, as those who go on to succeed.

The last time I saw Gretchen, she was being a kick a** mom, and jeeping in the sand dunes with her (3) sons. She was smiling, laughing, and from what I could tell - limitless.

When Jen, a San Diego teacher, told me she was getting up for her rowing club at 4:00am, I cheered her on, from a distance (my bed), and went back to sleep. Nearly a year later, her early bird rowing sessions expanded to 4x a week! What would generate such and cause it to stick?

Jen reports a cadre of motivators, including the God-like meditative experience, on the solitary smooth water, the sparkling lights in the distance, and the different birds. She expounds on the joy she experiences with a community of like minded "crazy people like me." And points out calling commands as a coxswain boosting her confidence. She describes feeling the life altering "power of the pause" when performing paddle arresting drills, which "caused me to slow down" and demonstrate skill.

She, reports, like Gretchen, going all in, researching, and studying YouTube videos, outside of class. And like we'll see later with Ellen, rather than viewing shortcoming as failure, she advocates it "built me up" and digs into challenge with a "we'll figure this out!" attitude.

Her activation happened, when she found herself going from "Oh, heck no! The only reason (to get up that early) is if my house is on fire or catching a flight" to "if you really want to do this . . . make this easier." So she went out and bought an old school alarm clock. She started laying her clothes out the night before, she went into full prep mode, which seems to "take the stress and possible panic away."

She feels these lessons transcend to other areas of her life and even something bigger than herself. She notes over and over, she'll mentally "re set" when challenged and remind herself "You've got this. This is practice. . . This is EXACTLY why we're out here. This is supposed to be fun."

Ellen, a human performance analyst and certified strength and conditioning coach, has seen her share of changemakers and stagnance in her highly sought after classes. Her observations include an attitude and a mindset that is clearly delineated between the "sarcastic and accepting" vs. the "complaining and hesitating." She also parsed out further a defeating "victim" type mentality, wherein responsibility to make change, seemed to be externalized. She defined this rationale as not having enough money for class, or enough time to work out, or sometimes, as blame deposited onto Ellen, herself.

She noted actual change anchoring in place when participants would observe their own changes and internalize them with "OMG I was consistent! I did what she said. I followed this goal. This is the new standard and I am never going back. THIS IS ME NOW. This is not momentary. This is life." And similar to Jen, she views shortcoming as "I have a lot of work to do!"

Whereas, those viewing the desire to change as temporary or a targeted chronological date, like a wedding, seemed to have blinders on and missed the bigger, richer, more rewarding picture. Also shame infused mindsets like "I suck. Why am I here? I am less than. I can't do it. I'm not good enough" signaled trouble.

Remember previous chapters discussing the narratives we chomp down on about ourselves, as facts. They need to be uprooted as quickly as possible.

Those viewing their metamorphosis as "life" and the "new standard" were also mindful of a wide range of unintended consequences, such as feeling more energized at work. In addition, their progress tethered to fueling their hobbies. One participant even noted enhanced testosterone levels, resulting in his wife's, once elusive, pregnancy. And those who discovered and brought her related material, initiating their own discovery, taking the ball and running, were also reverberating with success. She was able to detect a palpable change taking root, as students started offering "I lifted the (35) pound kettle bell today!" with a thrilled raised eyebrow and chipper fluctuation in tone.

Interestingly enough, both Gretchen and Ellen noted consequences, such as the threat of diabetes and death, were not the impetus for change. Threats, terror, and shame do not seem to be the way to motivate people. The old saying "The beatings will increase until morale improves" isn't the path to change. Think of the void your primary care doctors shout into, with repeated reminders such as "Cut down on smoking, under threat of lung cancer." Or "Reduce alcohol intake; it's a depressant, besides, it's full of sugar and calories." This does not seem to be the path to activating.

It's reminiscent of classic "carot versus stick" motivation. If you are "stick"ing yourself to force change and it's not sticking, consider instead to reach out for a carot that really means something you. Perhaps it is getting healthy enough, to be able to see your child make it to college.

You already know what is here on this side, for you. But what waits to be revealed on the other side of your particular challenge? Increased fertility? Increased God-like-meditative peace? More involved presence with your kids, in the sand dunes?

Internalizing and owning the change with a unique personal sovereignty, along with a deeper, richer reason than "I want my quads to pop through my jeans" appear to contribute to lasting change. Rather than terrorizing yourself with dismissive self talk and abandoning your wants and wishes, lean in, toward your limitless future.

Perhaps you are not "done" and "you're not doomed" to your current state, perhaps . . . you Just. Have. Work. To. Do.

Credit: Yvette Currie via CounselingSanDiego.Org

CHAPTER 10: OUR BIRTHRIGHT

"My purpose is to give them a rich and satisfying (abundant) life" John 10:10

The sun hasn't set on our time to thrive, here. Additionally, thriving or abundance doesn't just happen by accident. It is conscious. It is intentional. This process isn't about placing blame, either, neither offloading it onto others or getting bogged down in shame. It's about taking accountability where it is due and leaving the rest, that is not ours to shoulder. It is about looking at how we have engaged any of the unhealthy patterns described in this book through our attitudes, families, and churches. It is also about using this information as fuel for change, growth, and protection.

There may be obvious turning points. There may be barely perceptible cracks, that have grown bigger, over time. There may be insidious beliefs, wherein we never saw these rights as ours, in the first place. Perhaps assuming this abundance is for someone else or perhaps this isn't really what Jesus actually meant. Maybe it's all out there for everyone else, just specifically not for you. You may consider yourself "too injured" or "broken."

Remember, when conducting this 360 evaluation, observe the data like a curious scientist, not a judge. When we judge ourselves, we stifle the process of growth and getting to the other side. When we spend time asking ourselves "why" and "if only" and chiding ourselves, we lose the plot and can get stuck there. Instead, allow the data to surface, inspect it like a puzzle, shift the pieces around where necessary, and then move forward.

Identity

In the allegory of the baby elephant, the baby elephant, once held by chains, as a baby in training to be controlled and restrained, once reaching powerful adulthood size can be held by a string around it's ankle, still believing itself to be imprisoned.

Credit:Marie Currie via MarieCurrie1@gmail.com

The mind is still in captivity, despite actually being physically free. A mindset that is stuck, helpless, hopeless, and powerless, is a mind in captivity. As a gentle reminder these beliefs are not true.

This identity . . . is not for you.

Abundant Life

If you've never examined what this actually means, take the time to do it now. Write it down. Review it. Reflect on it. What does abundant life look like for you? Remember Proverbs 23:7

> *"For as he thinks in his heart, so is he."*

Carefully consider what you tell yourself about yourself and your birthright.

Study what captivity and freedom mean to you, in concrete terms. Question what actions and supports you'll need to actively break free. Honestly evaluate blocks to activation. Strategize proactive ways to clear the path to set yourself up for success.

Credit: Lola Russian via Pexels.com

1 John talks about anything that can take the place of God in our hearts, needs to be avoided. The Old Testament regularly discusses idols and how upsetting they were to God. I think idols can be people, when we fold ourselves into knots, altering our personalities, to avoid their anger. I think idols are also substances or anything else we allow to dictate our behaviors and hold us

hostage.

In Galatians 5:14

"For you have been called to live in freedom..."

Jesus wants us very much alive, in fact, "abundantly" so. His purpose for us is abundant and full of vitality and peace and joy. He wants us moving upward and in the direction of life.

Credit: Melvin Wahlin via Pexels.com

It's up to you to decide to execute.

* * *

Credit: Marie Currie via MarieCurrie1@gmail.com

CHAPTER 11: TIPS TO MELT CHURCH HURT

1. Discover, set, and hold those boundaries
2. Write
3. Box breathing
4. Directly address your concerns
5. Talk with a trusted other
6. Pray
7. Take action today

7. Rest

8. Exercise. How about daily?

9. Turn off your phone

10. Read your Bible mindfully

11. Meditative and mindfulness exercises

13. Tell yourself the truth. Let it set you free

14. Never cross the "I don't care what I say line" nor the "I don't care what I do" line

15. Distinguish between the bar of expectation and the bar of what actually is

16. Take the pause

17. Get some sunshine Vitamin D; God's natural immunity provision

18. Make it fun and get some jokes flowing

19. Check out that uplifting podcast

20. Read informative books

21. Give, volunteer, help

22. Consult with those who know more than you do

23. Do not ignore you gut

24. Promptly admit when you err

25. Actively seek solutions

26. Question the narrative

27. Interrupt the autopilot

28. Activate

EPILOGUE

"Do or Do Not. There is No Try." Yoda

BIBLIOGRAPHY

Adams, William E. *The Choices Program: How to Stop Hurting the People Who Love You.* William Adams, PhD, 2016.

Brown, Brene. *Daring Greatly: How the Courage to be Vulnerable Transforms the Way We Live, Love, Parent, and Lead.* New York: Gotham Books, 2012.

Csikszentmihalyi, Mihaly. *Flow: The Psychology of Optimal Experience.* New York: Harper Collins, 2009.

Cloud, Henry and Townsend, John. *Boundaries: When to Say Yes, How to Say No to Take Control of Your Life.* Grand Rapids: Zondervan, 1992.

Frankl, Viktor E. *Man's Search for Meaning.* Boston: Beacon Press, 1946.

Garcia et al., "Intermittent but not continuous access to cocaine produces individual variability in addiction susceptibility in rats." *Psychopharmacology* 237(10) (Oct):2929-2941. doi: 10.1007/s00213-020-05581-1.

Gonzalez, Anabel. *It's Not Me: Understanding Complex Trauma, Attachment, and Dissociation.* Anabel Gonzalez, 2018.

Gottman, John. *The Seven Principles for Making Marriage Work.* London, England: Orion, 1999.

Grover, Tim. *Relentless: From Good to Great to Unstoppable.* New York: Scribner, 2014.

Hawthorne, Nathaniel. *The Scarlet Letter*. Boston: Ticknor, Reed, & Fields, 1850.

Huber, Cheri. *There is Nothing Wrong with You: Going Beyond Self Hate*. Murphy's: Keep it Simple Books, 1997.

Katie, Byron "The Work." www.thework.com/instruction-the-work-byron-katie/.

Kyeong et al. "Effects of gratitude meditation on neural network functional connectivity and brain-heart coupling." *Scientific Reports* 7(1) (July 2017). DOI:10.1038/s41598-017-05520-9

Kiyosaki, Robert T. *Rich Dad Poor Dad*. Boston: Warner Books, 1997.

Miller, Alice. *For Your Own Good: Hidden Cruelty in Child-Rearing and the Roots of Violence*. New York: Noonday Press, 1990.

National Library of Medicine. List of Major Reasons for Divorce by Individuals and Couples Who Participated in PREP.

New Living Translation Bible. NLT Online. https://www.tyndale.com/sites/nlt/, 1996.

Pearcey, Nancy. *The Toxic War on Masculinity: How Christianity Reconciles the Sexes*. Ada: Baker Publishing Group, 2023.

Peck, M. Scott. *People of the Lie: The Hope for Healing Human Evil*. New York: Simon and Schuster, 1983.

Price, Catherine. *How to Break Up with Your Phone*. New York: Ten Speed Press, 2018.

Santos, Laurie. "Achieve More Happiness, Improve Well-Being and Optimize Performance." Featured speaker presentation, Navy

SEAL Foundation Impact Forum, San Diego, CA, October 17, 2022.

Twenge, Jean. *iGen: Why Today's Super Connected Kids are Growing up Less Rebellious, More Tolerant, Less Happy - and Completely Unprepared for Adulthood -and What that Means for the Rest of Us.* New York: Atria, 2018.

Willink, Jocko. *Discipline Equals Freedom: Field Manual Mk1-MOD1*. New York: St. Martin's Press, 2020.

World Population Review. "Child Trafficking by Country 2023." https://worldpopulationreview.com/country-rankings/child-trafficking-by-country.

ABOUT THE AUTHOR

Yvette Currie, L M F T

Yvette Currie has been in the field of Psychology for over 20 years. She is a licensed clinician with her own private practice in San Diego, California and can be contacted through CounselingSanDiego.Org.

She's treated a spectrum of challenges, from inside safehouses, youth treatment facilities, offender programs, to human trafficking. She's trained military personnel, on resilience, while deploying alongside them. She also held a position as a professor at National University, training up and coming therapists.

She consults with people to recognize, no matter where any of us have been, pain is pain, and we all have the capacity to be restored. And then take it to the next level.

Her cosmopolitan lifestyle, as a citizen of the world, includes previously residing in Japan and New Zealand. These experiences continue to contribute to her unique perspective and voice. Combined with this, she happens to be a PK (Preacher's Kid), with a lifetime of church and ministry experience.

She's been known to compete in Toastmasters International, foosball, or fantasy football, on occasion.

www.ingramcontent.com/pod-product-compliance
Lightning Source LLC
LaVergne TN
LVHW010904110826
845149LV00005B/1469

* 9 7 9 8 9 8 8 6 8 5 5 0 0 *